Contents

Page 7: Ravel, *Bolero*
Reproduced by permission of Editions Durand S. A., Paris/G. Ricordi & Co. (London) Ltd.

Page 16: Ravel, *Pavan for a dead Infanta*
Reproduced by permission of Editions Max Eschig, Paris/G. Ricordi & Co. (London) Ltd.

Introduction

Welcome to *Music Theory in Practice Model Answers*, Grade 1. These answers are a useful resource to help you prepare for ABRSM Theory of Music exams. This book is designed to be used alongside the revised *Music Theory in Practice* workbook (published 2008).

All the answers in this book would receive full marks in an exam. Accepted options are included for cases where an answer may be expressed in more than one way. For composition-style questions, a model answer is provided as an example of good practice.

Using these answers

- Answers are given in the same order and, where possible, in the same layout as in the corresponding *Music Theory in Practice* workbook. This makes it easy to match the answers to the questions.
- Where it is necessary to show the answer on a stave, the original stave is printed in grey with the answer shown in black, for example:

- Alternative answers are separated by an oblique stroke (/) or by *or*, for example:

B / B♮ / B natural

- Answers that require the candidate to write out a scale or chord have been shown at one octave only. Reasonable alternatives at different octaves can also receive full marks.

First published in 2009 by ABRSM (Publishing) Ltd, a wholly owned subsidiary of ABRSM
Reprinted in 2010, 2011, 2012

© 2009 by The Associated Board of the Royal Schools of Music

Typeset by Barnes Music Engraving Ltd
Cover by Økvik Design
Inside design by Vermillion
Printed in England by Caligraving Ltd, Thetford, Norfolk

MIX
Paper from responsible sources
FSC
www.fsc.org   FSC™ C109619

Time values

Exercise 1 ✔ o Name semibreve (whole note)

𝅗𝅥 Name minim (half note)

♩ Name crotchet (quarter note)

♪ Name quaver (eighth note)

Exercise 2 ✔ A o lasts as long as 4 ♩

A o lasts as long as 2 𝅗𝅥

A 𝅗𝅥 lasts as long as 4 ♪

A ♩ lasts as long as 2 ♪

Bar-lines and time signatures

Exercise 1 ✔ bar-lines
a double bar-line

Exercise 2 ✔ time signatures

Exercise 3 ✔ how many beats in a bar
the type of beats in a bar – the 4 represents crotchet (quarter-note) beats
2 crotchet (quarter-note) beats in a bar
3 crotchet (quarter-note) beats in a bar

Exercise 4 ✔ 𝄴

Exercise 5 ✔

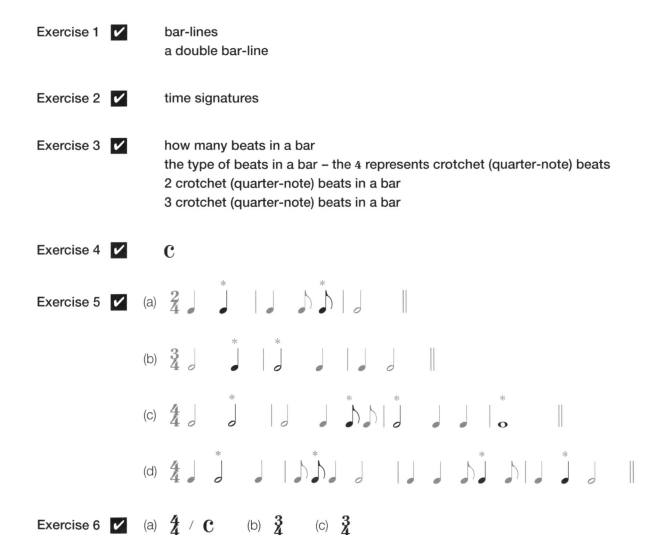

Exercise 6 ✔ (a) $\frac{4}{4}$ / 𝄴   (b) $\frac{3}{4}$ (c) $\frac{3}{4}$

Notes on the stave

Exercise 1 ✔

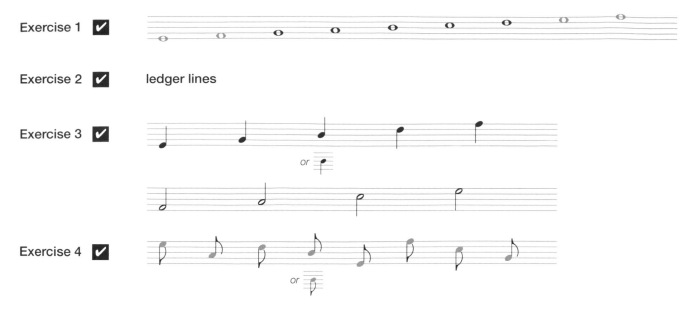

Exercise 2 ✔ ledger lines

Exercise 3 ✔

Exercise 4 ✔

The treble (G) clef

Exercise 1 ✔

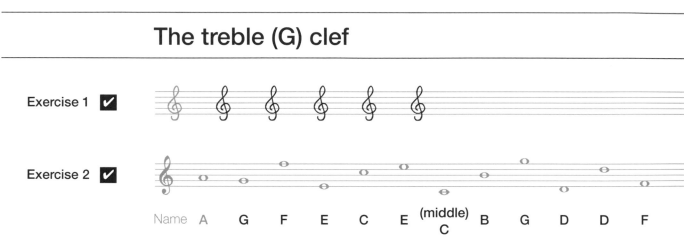

Exercise 2 ✔

Name	A	G	F	E	C	E	(middle) C	B	G	D	D	F

The bass (F) clef

Exercise 1 ✔

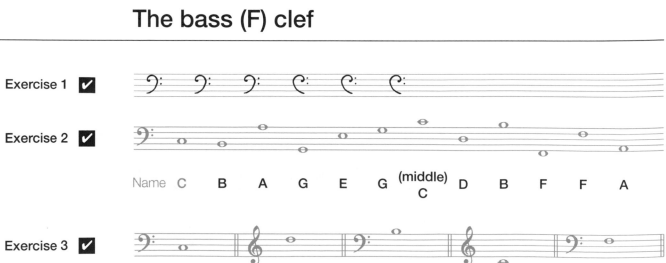

Exercise 2 ✔

Name	C	B	A	G	E	G	(middle) C	D	B	F	F	A

Exercise 3 ✔

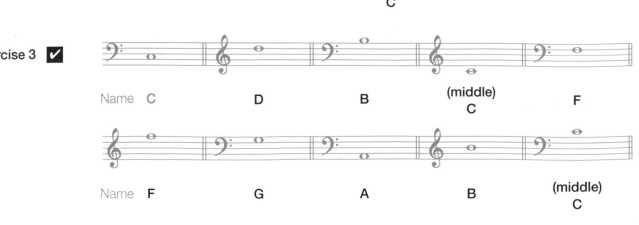

Name	C	D	B	(middle) C	F

Name	F	G	A	B	(middle) C

Exercise 4 ✔

More on time values

Exercise 1 ✔ semiquaver (16th note)

Exercise 2 ✔ (a)  (c)

(b)  (d)

Exercise 3 ✔ (c)

(a) (d)

(b)  (e)

Rests

Exercise 1 ☑

Exercise 2 ☑ (a)

(b)

(c)

Ties

Exercise 1 ☑

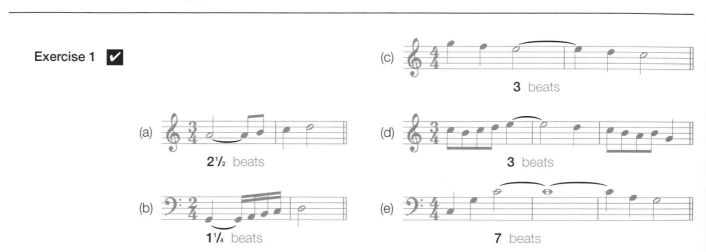

(a) 2½ beats

(b) 1¼ beats

(c) 3 beats

(d) 3 beats

(e) 7 beats

Dots

Exercise 1 ☑

A 𝅗𝅥. lasts as long as 6 ♪

A 𝅘𝅥. lasts as long as 3 ♪

A 𝅗𝅥. lasts as long as 1½ 𝅗𝅥

A ♪. lasts as long as 3 ♪

A 𝅗𝅥. lasts as long as 12 ♪

Accidentals

Exercise 1 ✔

sharp
raises the note by one semitone
flat
lowers the note by one semitone
natural
raises or lowers the note by one semitone / cancels a preceding accidental / acts as a
cautionary reminder to cancel a preceding accidental

Exercise 2 ✔ (a)  (b)  (c)

(d)  (e)

Exercise 3 ✔ (a) 1 : G♯   2 : G   3 : B♭   4 : B♮   5 : B   6 : A
         (b) 1 : C   2 : B♭   3 : C♯   4 : C   5 : B   6 : G
         (c) 1 : F   2 : F♯   3 : D   4 : B♭   5 : B   6 : F

Semitones and tones

Exercise 1 ✔

Exercise 2 ✔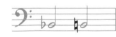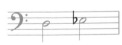

  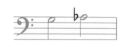 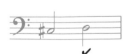

Exercise 3 ✔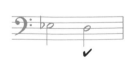

Exercise 6 (a)

Cancelling an accidental

Exercise 1 (a)

Exercise 2 (a) 1 : C   2 : B♭   3 : B♮   4 : G   5 : B♭   6 : F
            (b) 1 : D   2 : G♯   3 : G   4 : F♯   5 : C♮   6 : C♯

Degrees of the scale and intervals

Exercise 1

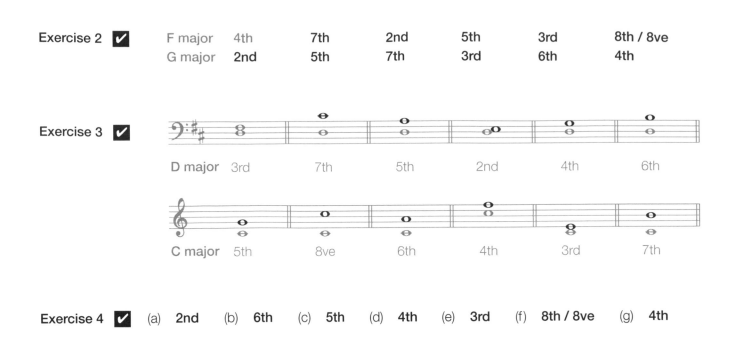

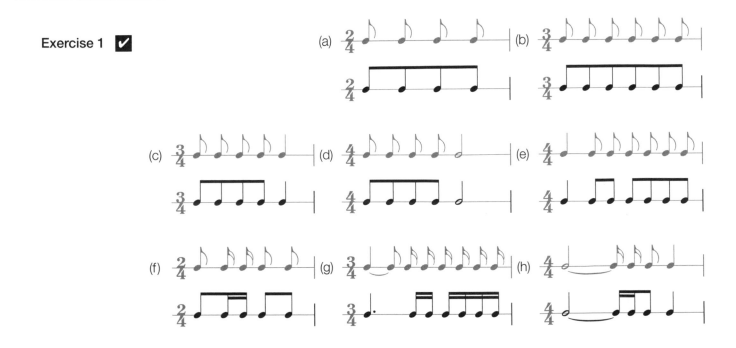

The tonic triad

Composing an answering rhythm

Exercise 2 ✔   There are many ways of completing this exercise. The specimen answers that follow provide examples of good practice.

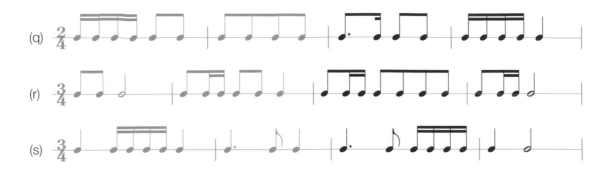

General exercises

Exercise 1 ✔ (a) walking pace / medium speed

(b) $\frac{3}{4}$
3 crotchet (quarter-note) beats in a bar

(c) a dotted minim (dotted half note) is worth 3 crotchets (quarter notes) and will fill a bar in $\frac{3}{4}$ time

(d) piano
play quietly / softly

(e) 3rd

(f) E
D

(g) semiquaver (16th note)

(h)

1	2	3	4
☐	☐	✔	☐

(i)

1	2	3	4
✔	☐	☐	☐

(j)

True	False
✔	☐

(k) accent / stress the note

(l)

Exercise 2 ✔ (a) quick / fast / cheerful

(b) C major

(c) $\frac{4}{4}$

(d) slurs
play the notes smoothly

(e) play the note staccato / short and detached

(f)
1	2	3	4
☐	✔	☐	☐

(g) 2

(h) crotchet (quarter-note) rest

(i)
True	False
☐	✔

(j)
A	B	C	D	E	F	G
☐	☐	☐	☐	☐	☐	✔

(k) the rhythm is the same

(l)

Exercise 3 ✔ (a) slow / leisurely

(b) diminuendo
getting (gradually) softer / quieter

(c) 1, 2, 6

(d) 56 crotchet (quarter-note) beats in a minute

(e) smoothly

(f) *pp*

(g) 3 and 7

(h) 5

(i) ———< getting (gradually) louder

>——— getting (gradually) quieter / softer

(j)

1	2		3	4	5
☐	✔	or	✔	☐	☐

Either answer (above) is acceptable as bars 3 and 7 both contain crotchet (quarter) notes, yet bar 8 contains crotchet (quarter) notes and a crotchet (quarter-note) rest.

(k)

A	B♭	C	D	E	F
☐	☐	☐	☐	✔	☐

(l) B♮ / B flat

Dvořák

Exercise 4 ✔

(a) treble

(b) **G major**

(c)

(d) **3rd**

(e) **F♯ / F sharp**

(f)
1	2	3	4	5
☐	☐	☐	✔	☐

(g) **1, 3, 4, 5**

(h)
smooth	loud	quiet	slow	fast	merry	sad
✔	☐	✔	✔	☐	☐	☐

(i)
A	B	C	D	E	F♯	G
☐	☐	✔	☐	☐	☐	☐

(j)
True	False
✔	☐

(k)